THINKABOUT
Touching

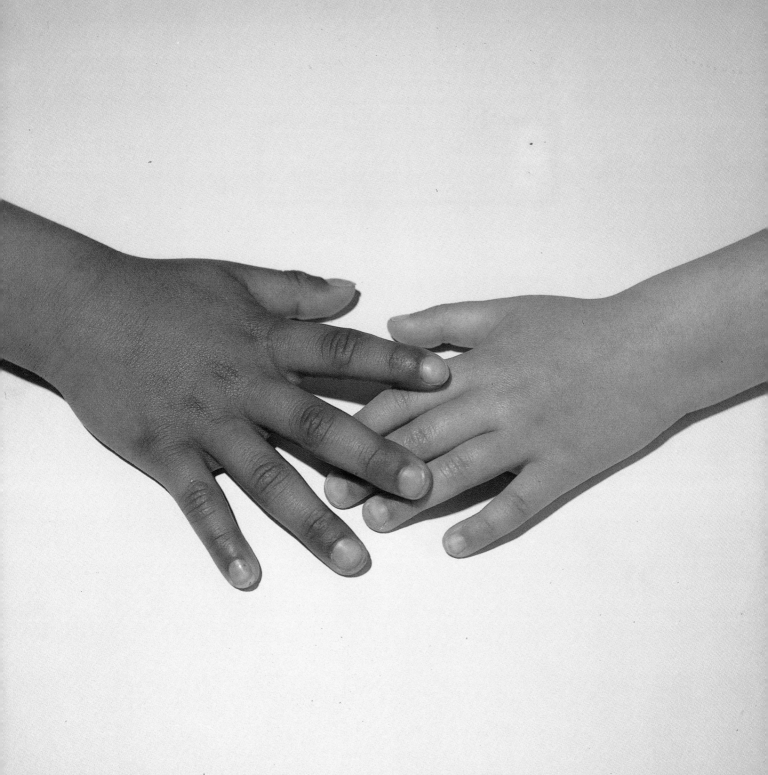

THINKABOUT
Touching

Text: Henry Pluckrose
Photography: Chris Fairclough

Franklin Watts
London/New York/Sydney/Toronto

© 1985 Franklin Watts Limited
12A Golden Square
London W1

ISBN : 0 86313 276 6

Editor : Ruth Thomson
Design : Edward Kinsey

Typesetting : Keyspools

Printed in Belgium

About this book

This book is designed for use in the home, playgroup, kindergarten and infant school.

Parents can share the book with young children. Its aim is to bring into focus some of the elements of life and living which are all too often taken for granted. To develop fully, all young children need to have their understanding of the world deepened and the language they use to express their ideas extended. This book, and others in the series, takes the everyday things of the child's world and explores them, harnessing curiosity and wonder in a purposeful way.

For those working with young children each book is designed to be used both as a picture book, which explores ideas and concepts, and as a starting point to talk and exploration. The pictures have been selected because they are of interest in themselves and also because they include elements which will promote enquiry. Talk can lead to displays of items and pictures collected by children and teacher. Pictures and collages can be made by the children themselves.

Everything in our environment is of interest to the growing child. The purpose of these books is to extend and develop that interest.

Henry Pluckrose.

Move your hand gently
over the page.
Is it rough or smooth,
hot or cold,
wet or dry?

What do you like to touch –
the smoothness
of wood,

the roughness
of brick,

the grittiness
of sand,

the slipperiness
of clay?

What do you like to touch –
soft things

or hard things?

Do you like to touch
the roughness of tree bark,

the smoothness
of glass?

Do you like the tingle
of cold snow,

the warmth of water?

What things are
most fun to touch –
street railings,

corrugated card,

sticky paint,

wet soap,

autumn leaves,

smooth pebbles?

Have you ever felt
the sharpness
of a thorn,

the prickliness
of holly,

the softness
of feathers,

the jaggedness
of broken rock,

the smoothness
of eggshell,

the roughness of towelling?

Can you imagine
what it would be like
to touch the trunk
of an elephant,

or the tongue of a cat?

Look around you.
What things do you like
touching the most?
What things do you like
touching the least?

PRINTED IN BELGIUM BY
proost
INTERNATIONAL BOOK PRODUCTION